THE ENERGY SELF-DEFENSE SERIES - No. 4

ANNI & CARSTEN SENNOV

ENERGY
SELF-DEFENSE
for
LOVE COUPLES

good adventures publishing

Energy Self-Defense
for Love Couples

©2018, Anni & Carsten Sennov and Good Adventures Publishing
First edition, second impression
Set with Cambria
Layout: Anni Sennov – www.sennovpartners.com
Cover design: Michael Bernth – www.monovoce.dk
Author photo: Aamod & Sophelia Korhonen - www.balanceisjoy.com

ISBN 978-87-7206-003-3

Contents

Notice

When reading this book please be in a spirit of open-mindedness.

Although the authors and the publisher have made every effort to ensure the accuracy and completeness of information contained in this book, we assume no responsibility for errors, inaccuracies, omissions, or any inconsistencies herein. Any offense caused to people, places, or organizations is unintentional.

Readers should use their own judgment, or consult a holistic medical expert or their personal physician for specific applications to their individual problems.

Welcome

Love can take on many forms of emotion. We love our parents, children, and spouse in different ways. In this book, we will be focusing on the love energy between you and your significant other. It would benefit you greatly if both you and your partner read this book.

Love is a very popular topic. Most people love to read about love, especially if the love story ends well. However, this Energy Self-Defense guide for Love Couples is not a love story. It will offer you advice on how to make your love story become a good experience that lasts, so it only ends if you want it to, or because there is a poor match between you and your partner.

Ask anyone and they will probably agree that it's difficult to define exactly what love means to them. In fact, modern, conscious people often end up in a situation where they choose to stay in an unsatisfying relationship even though, deep in their heart, they want to leave.

By reading this book you will hopefully get a good feel for what love means to you and where your boundaries are, as well as how high you value love in your relationship and daily life. We hope that you will benefit in your love relationship from the Energy Self-Defense tools described in this book.

Love is worth fighting for but love is not supposed to be a fight itself. Therefore, you should learn how to defend, protect and balance your own energy even when you are together with the one you love.

Enjoy reading!
Anni & Carsten Sennov

What is love?

Love is natural and not something that can be easily taught. The only way to get access to the love that is found deep inside yourself is to be true and honest to yourself, be full of joy, and pay respect to both yourself, others and to life. Then love will be revealed from deep inside of you as if it was the most natural thing in the whole world.

You've heard of the expression "love is in the air". It's easy to see and feel when there is a strong love present. When you're in love you just know it and it's impossible for you to explain why you love a certain person and why you feel an urge to embrace them with all your love. It's an inner feeling that makes you want to show your affection for the person you love, whether it's your spouse, children, family, friends, or even people you don't know on a personal level. It's actually possible to love people you have never even met because of who they are, how much they have contributed to help others, or because of what they have accomplished in life.

Attraction, on the other hand, is always related to external factors, including appearance, and physical and sexual chemistry.

Sex and attraction are usually very closely related in a love couple relationship. It's the combination of love and seduction that is so very special and powerful in most love couple relationships all over the world, unless the local culture indicates something different.

If you love someone unconditionally, it can be difficult and also irrelevant to point out exactly what it is about the person that you love the most, because that is not important.

What's important is that you love the person wholeheartedly or profoundly even though you might be attracted to some very specific characteristics of theirs.

Are you in love with your spouse?

When love couples have lived together for many years, they tend to forget to distinguish between the concepts of love, which set people free, and attraction, which keeps people devoted and sometimes imprisoned by one another. Love can be the binding force in their relationship, although it should set them free and allow both of them to express who they really are as individuals.

Many love couples have simply become so accustomed to the presence of each other in daily life that they take each other for granted and don't pay attention to each other's personal needs anymore. Life has become routine, and so has the relationship. So as the years pass by, they both risk losing more and more contact with their original personality and they may actually end up losing themselves in their relationship.

There is a difference between loving a person and being in love. If you love a person whom you initially were very attracted to, you might also risk losing yourself, if you end up staying in your relationship even when you don't find your spouse particularly attractive anymore. In fact, many love couples end up changing their original personality after spending many years together as spouses, because they have influenced and assumed each other's behavior so much, that they have lost contact with their own true self, which can be both good and bad.

Have you grown apart because you spent time following different life paths and therefore have nothing in common except for your children? If you don't make efforts to stay updated on each other's energies, or have sex on a regular basis, then it's very difficult to feel connected in the long run. You simply end up being strangers to one another.

Do you live in such a relationship, or have you totally forgotten to prioritize your spouse and your relationship in daily life because you have countless other things to take care of every day?

Do you love your spouse deeply and wish that you could spend much more time together, or are you tired of him/her and the way the relationship works?

Either way, it's important to sort and balance your personal energy and the energies in your relationship, so you can make a definitive choice about whether to stay together or not, and how much energy you should invest in your relationship on a daily, weekly or monthly basis.

How deep and strong is your love and do you feel satisfied in your relationship? Ask yourself, has the love and attraction totally disappeared?

To be able to thrive in your relationship, it's very important that you answer these questions in an honest way. If you are not sure about what you feel, it's even more important to balance your personal energy and make use of the Energy Self-Defense tools that we share with you in this energy guide, so you can get closer to your inner truth and be totally honest with yourself, your partner and your relationship.

Being honest with yourself

If you keep convincing yourself that things are different than they actually are, and you don't want to relate to reality as it is, nor to your inner truth, then this book might not be for you. You should not start using any of the energy tools in this book if you are not willing to face the truth; specifically, your own inner spiritual truth.

If you are honest with yourself and your partner from the very beginning of your relationship, you obviously run the risk that the relationship will soon end if you don't agree with each other. However, this is much better than not facing reality in order to adapt to your love partner. Honesty creates a very strong foundation for you as a love couple to build your life upon.

If you are always honest with yourself and choose to only do what feels right for you with respect to your love partner, both of you will always have freedom in your relationship. Freedom is what makes the creativity level stay high, so you keep on inspiring and surprising each other in a good way.

Don't be afraid of loving others

Love is **never** complicated. Human attraction is!!!

It's only in people's minds that there are a lot of demands attached to love, but in Spirit there isn't.

What does it mean to love someone unconditionally? When you love another person, you hope they reciprocate, and if not you can still show true altruism and love them no matter what.

A human love relationship is usually a low-frequency physical version of a high-frequency divine love relationship. Therefore, love sometimes has difficulty finding its way into people's hearts and bodies due to their basic physical behavior and needs such as lust, greed, selfishness, violence, control, hunger for power, manipulation, etc. It's therefore of great importance that you don't hand over the power of your life to other people, just because you love them, because they might not be able to handle your energy in the way you want them to and you may end up feeling powerless and frustrated in your relationship.

There is absolutely nothing wrong in loving other people unconditionally. It's in fact a very beautiful gesture. Just don't be naive and hand over full responsibility and control of your life to them.

If they don't embrace you with love in the same way that you embrace them, then your feeling of love will usually disappear over time. When there is a feeling of mutually unconditional love, you don't need to do anything but to delight or cherish each other, because by doing that you will always support each other and there will be no room whatsoever for control in your life.

Love and freedom always join and support each other, as love creates the basis for human freedom and vice versa.

When you follow your heart, and allow yourself the utmost level of freedom with love and respect for yourself and others around you, you will get a 3-in-1 good feeling consisting of love, freedom and joy.

By giving control over your life to those you love, love will usually be replaced with authority, because that is what you give attention to by wanting your partner, for example, to make decisions on your behalf, and control represents a much lower frequency and human quality than pure love.

So if you want unconditional love to be a part of your daily life, then start radiating love in your own life and don't be naive. Listen to your heart, spirit and body to make sure everything feels fine deep down in every cell. Listen to your own intuition and body, so that every relation you are involved in is good for you on all levels.

If you get the slightest feeling of having to deliver something that doesn't feel right for you, or if you must trespass your own personal boundaries to satisfy another person, you are actually about to give away a part of your soul and spirit. Don't ever give love and positive energy to others in the hope of getting something back, because you never know what you will get back. If bad energy should find its way into your system, it can be a long and painful road to get rid of it again.

If you love unconditionally, you should never be afraid of loving others, because love comes from deep within yourself and is spread out to the world and to others from your inner spiritual core. All the love that you radiate will always come back to you in your daily life, because love attracts love. However, you might not receive love from those you send it to, so don't be disappointed if you instead get it from other people.

Longing for love
doesn't give you love

If you are longing for love from other people, the feeling of yearning will radiate through your aura and this doesn't give you love.

Love comes from the inside of your divine source and when you radiate love, other people who also do so will feel attracted to you. It doesn't mean that mutual love automatically creates the basis for a love relationship between you. Maybe instead you will end up being best friends.

If you long for love and if you don't know how true love feels deep inside, you will not be fully able to see and sense whether you are actually being loved or not. Maybe you are just playing a physical role in another person's life by supporting them with whatever they need. However, the closer you get to your own inner feeling of love, the more visible your role will be in your relationship. So, if the relationship isn't good for you, you will soon find out and maybe not in a good way, but in a way that will make you wake up to reality very quickly.

Most other people usually expect that you know what love is and that you understand your own role in your love relationship right from the beginning, but it isn't always easy to see things clearly in life if you are totally in love. It takes time to wake up to reality, and it usually takes a much longer time if you have been longing for love for a very long time. So be patient with yourself.

Listen to all of the good advice that you get from others and enjoy the feeling of being loved right now, even if it doesn't last. Love is for sure an amazing feeling even if the attraction and the relationship don't last forever.

Most importantly don't be scared of being hurt. There is a risk in everything and also in committing to a love relationship, and if you don't take the risk then you won't have the opportunity of finding love.

Always sort your energy even when you are with your spouse

(1 mantra)

Just as you take care to brush your teeth every day, it's good to get into the habit of sorting your energies in your relationship, as well as in your family, and make sure that you remember to take care of your own energy every day.

Unfortunately, many people refuse to accept that their loved ones, and especially their spouse or partner, are energy thieves. It may be hard for them to realize that they do not have the perfect partner or a partner who loves them unconditionally. A person who loves you unconditionally would never try to get hold of your energy or steal it from you by trying to get your full attention all the time and/or creating drama in your life. They would rather set you free and support you in whatever choices you make in life, knowing that you would do the same for them.

However, the bigger issues for you is not that you have an energy thief around you. The problem is that you get so used to giving away your energy to other people who want it, and soon you have no energy left for yourself. You can in fact train other people to become energy thieves without knowing it, because you nurse and feed them with energy all the time, and when they lack it, they will automatically seek you out for more.

This **cannot** be the result of loving other people too much, because you **cannot** love other people too much. However, you can give them **too much** attention all the time, and not many people can handle such large amounts of energy without feeling like a king, or queen or a celebrity, if they have lots of energy themselves. There will thus be an overload in their energy system which can cause trouble, especially for those who love them. For example, the person with the extra energy might become controlling or manipulative etc. in their relationships with others.

This is also a good thing to teach your children, because during their lives they will have relationships with close friends and boy- and girlfriends, and one day they may get married and will have to take care of their own energy while being in a love relationship.

You can easily sort and balance your own energy by saying this mantra:

"I now pull all my rightful energy
back to myself from 'X'
– in a cleansed form –
and I send the energy of 'X'
out of my own energy field
and return it to him/her."

If you are a person who loves to embrace everybody around you and you think a lot about other people and how you can best meet their needs, even when you are not together, then you risk giving them too much attention – and too much energy; energy that they might not use in the way you hoped for, either because they can't or they won't. This is often what will disappoint you the most in your relationships with others: giving them a gift in the form of energy and attention that they use for another purpose than what you had originally intended.

Be aware that all of the energy and attention that you give away is no longer yours once you give it away, so you cannot decide how someone else should use it.

Whether you like it or not, you must accept that all people have different perceptions in life, and just because people are related to and love each other, they might not want to do the exact same things in the exact same way. What is there to explore and discuss with someone who thinks in the exact same way as you do? What should you talk about? How can you be inspired by each other if you are exactly alike?

Just think about it, most relationships are based on a foundation where you can exchange energies with each other in a balanced way. If you are totally alike, there is nothing to exchange and then you don't need them in your life and they don't need you, simply because you will eventually get bored when being together with people where you have nothing else to share but love.

When you sort energies after spending time together with other people, whether it's your spouse, your family/family in law, friends, colleagues, neighbors or others, nobody will lose their own energy. Instead, they are inspired by being together and will be filled up with good experiences on top of their own energy, which is what most people search for when socializing with others.

This is in fact how things should be when people are together in a love relationship, and in all other contexts.

Worship your love relationship
(1 mantra)

It's very important on a regular basis to show your love partner how grateful you are for your relationship. Besides loving your partner, it's actually a big thing for a love couple to be able to live together every day. Not all people who love each other have this opportunity in life for different reasons. So you should really worship being able to live together as a love couple.

If your love partner is low on energy, you can send him/her tons of love and embrace him/her with your love and fill up their whole being with your love. This is especially helpful if your love partner is very busy or stressed, because there is nothing in life that is so beautiful and life affirming as unconditional love between two people, whether it's between love couples or between a parent and a child, etc.

There is absolutely nothing wrong in supporting your love partner wholeheartedly and showering them with all your love, if you know that the love and energy will be used in a good way. In that case you don't need to sort and balance your energies when your love partner is back on top of things, because he/she will be forever grateful and send tons of love back to you, and will always support you whenever you need it.

When you want to share your love and gratefulness with your love partner, it's easily done by using the following energy mantra. You can think or say it quietly or out loud, and your love partner doesn't have to be around you to feel your strong love. They can in fact be on the other side of the Earth and you can still be sure that the energy will reach them and go directly to their heart:

*"I now embrace my love partner
and fill him/her up with all my love,
and I embrace myself and our love relationship
with all my love,
so we both feel loved and feel grateful
for being together as a love couple."*

This is a very strong energy manifestation that will be felt strongly by your love partner and yourself, and others who are close to you. It's not an energy manifestation that you should send out to keep your love partner to yourself, but to instead show unconditional love to him/her. It's actually a very personal "thing" between the two of you that doesn't involve others. Not even your children.

We are all influenced by our past

(2 mantras)

Everyone has a past either as individuals or as a couple, which might influence and shape them in negative ways as they begin a new relationship. Using the Energy Self-Defense tools in this book can be of great help in your relationship.

If you are so lucky to meet your soul or spirit mate, you might not think that you need much guidance from this book, because everything is fine in your relationship. When a couple feels that they recognize or know each other from somewhere else the very first time they meet they usually have a very strong spiritual connection with each other. In this case, there is not much that needs to be explained, because love is their guiding star in their relationship.

If you want to understand more about your spirit mate, we recommend that you read our book *"Spirit Mates – the New Time Relationship"*.

You can also learn more on this powerful topic in our book *"SPIRIT MATES – How to Find Your Soul Mate Version 2.0 – Your Ultimate Love Partner"*, which has 10 real life spirit mates love stories in it. This book explains the remarkable benefits and what is so unique about living together with your spirit mate.

Many people however, don't have this definitive feeling of love for each other when they first meet. They typically begin with attraction and start from scratch in getting to know each other, simply because they don't have this deep inner feeling of unconditional love for each other when they first meet. Their mutual love will instead grow stronger as time passes by.

When young people first get together as a couple, they tend to bring their parents' perception and views on cohabitation, security, economics and sex with them into their own relationship. This is simply because their parents are their role models in life up to that point in time. If they have been in a relationship before, they will also be influenced by their previous experiences, and will therefore bring memories and certain ways of doing things with them into their new relationship.

The same goes for adults who meet a new love partner. They always bring their past into their new love relationship, and doing so can influence the outcome of the new relationship in both good and bad ways. We therefore recommend that you clean all energies from the past that you have brought with you into your new relationship, no matter your age.

It is helpful to reflect on the past and gain understanding so that you can begin your new relationship with clarity. You should not dwell on the past when you live in the present, but bring the best with you from the past into the present and get rid of the rest. It's not healthy to have a lot of unresolved details from past relationships mixed in with your new relationship, as this could muddy the waters in your new relationship.

If your body has not let go of the past you can't succeed, because some of your energy is tied up in things and experiences that happened before you and your partner met. Therefore, it's of the utmost importance that both of you learn how to deal with the past in a balanced way, so it doesn't impact your current and future relationships.

Sex has a great impact on the intimacy of your relationship, so if you have little or no sex in the relationship, this doesn't allow you to be close to each other's energy and create proximity and intimacy where you share everything with each other. When having sex, you both release some of your old emotional tensions that are stored in the body memory deep down at the cellular level from your respective lives before you met each other.

To effectively relieve emotional and mental tensions and all sorts of limitations from your past before you and your partner met, even if you have been in a relationship for a long time, you can use the following two Energy Self-Defense mantras. Say the following sentences in your head or picture them taking place:

"I now pull back all my rightful energy to myself
from 'X' and from everybody else in my past
– in a cleansed form –
and I send the rightful energy of 'X'
and everybody else in my past
out of my own energy field
and return it to them."

and

"I now forgive myself and 'X'
and everybody else
for what happened,
and I forgive myself,
because I have kept the tensions,
sadness, aggression and frustration in me
that was created in my past.
I now let go of all negative things
that happened in my past
and create space for new
positive experiences in my life."

Previous relationships' impact on your current relationship

(5 mantras)

Did you know that the most powerful way of exchanging and transferring energy between two people is taking place during intercourse? This is especially true when there is an exchange of bodily fluids, because there are large amounts of energy in sperm and body fluids. If the couple loves each other deeply and there is a good balance between them, then a spiritual spark is lit when they have sex, which empowers their inner life force so they can exchange even more energy with each other.

This means that when you are looking back on your past relationship(s), you will also have exchanged large amounts of energy with your previous partner(s), which is something you should be conscious about. Perhaps you have given much more energy to them than you have received back.

If your previous relationship(s) have been equal and balanced, then the energy exchange between you has most certainly been in balance. Since there was a purpose of the exchange itself, you both have come out as winners and have learned a lot from the relationship and from each other. In such cases there will be no outstanding energy issues, since you should each use the energy exchange to move on in your respective lives.

Unbalanced conditions, however, require a lot of energy from you, which you can sort out, because you probably lack some of your personal energy that was meant to be used in your future life and not on a previous "one-way energy" partner.

Lack of energy can create imbalances in your body and mind and can perpetuate feeling empty inside, because you don't have the same power as before. You may also have a new behavior that is not really yours because of transferred energy from a previous partner. This might have changed you in a way that was not intended when the energy exchange took place, and the result is that you no longer have the same potential as before.

In some past relationships, it was everyday life itself that was energy consuming because of negative discussions, accusations, etc., and you might have even caused or sent out some of this negative energy yourself. Nevertheless, it's important for you to bring balance into the situation even if it happened many years ago, so you can get your own energy back and use it now and in the future.

Even if the relationship itself was balanced, the break-up could have been unbalanced with things ending badly, so you still have some outstanding energy to sort out in order to get back to becoming fully balanced in your current life.

Often a very hard and violent break-up between you and your ex-partner will have been a part of the actual energy sorting process, as the two parties don't want to have anything to do with each other anymore, and they therefore try to get rid of each other's energy, making the actual "cleaning process" extra powerful.

The couples where both parties manage to break up in a loving way after being in a balanced relationship don't have any energy issues, since both have realized and accepted that they should not be together and that their lives go in different directions.

Because there are many ways to break up, your energy can

be stuck in your past relationship(s), so if you want to get all your outstanding energy back to yourself and you want to balance, dissolve and send away all negative energies from your past relationship(s), use these Energy Self-Defense mantras:

Step 1: Sort your energies

First you should sort your energies so that you separate your own energy from any previous partner and allow yourself to stand even stronger in your own energy than you do now. Repeat the energy sorting mantra as many times a day as you like:

"I now pull all my rightful energy back to myself
from my ex-partner(s)
– in a cleansed form –
and I send all the rightful energy of my ex-partner(s)
out of my own energy field
and return it to them."

Step 2: Dissolve all bad energies between you

By embracing yourself and your ex-partner(s) with white light/energy you cleanse out all negative energies that have ever existed between you:

"I now embrace myself and my ex-partner(s)
in a pure white light/energy
to dissolve all bad energies between us."

Step 3: Forgive yourself

It's very important that you forgive yourself and your ex-partner(s) for what happened and let go of the past, which will happen when using this mantra:

"I now forgive myself and my ex-partner(s)
for what happened.
I now let go of all that happened
and create space for new
positive experiences in my life."

If you have been involved in one or more tough relationships where it's difficult for you to forget what happened and let go of the past, and where you don't feel free inside despite using the previous Energy Self-Defense mantras many times a day, you can separate your energies by using this mantra:

"I now place a thick wall
of blue boundary-setting energy
between me and my ex-partner(s)
to separate our energies
and to keep my ex-partner(s) away from me."

If you have a feeling or know for sure that your ex-partner(s) have spread out your energy to others in their network or to a new partner and family, you should also pull back your energy from your ex-partner's network and from their whole life, so you can be sure that you don't miss anything because they gave it away to somebody else.

Your energy is your rightful energy and it should always be around you and not around somebody else no matter who they are. Not even your children should walk around with your energy, as they have their own often stronger energy.

So, when you say these energy sorting mantras, always start focusing on your ex-partner(s) and then say the mantras again where you include their network, etc.:

"I now pull all my rightful energy back to myself
from my ex-partner(s)
and from their network or from whomever
they shared my energy with
– in a cleansed form –
and I send all the rightful energy of my ex-partner(s)
out of my own energy field
and return it to them."

Are you happy

(4 mantras)

There are so many things that can influence your relationship in a negative way and there are so many ways to lose your energy and be unhappy. It's therefore important to consult your inner voice and ask yourself if you are happy in your relationship.

This book cannot make you happier if you are not pleased with how your life is. It can, however, help you to balance your own energy in your body, mind and in your relationship, as well as balancing the energy between you as a couple. However, it's up to each of you to decide whether or not you are happy when being together as a couple.

The main questions to consider are whether or not you love each other, and if you are satisfied with how things are in your relationship or not. If not, you should change things and spend time figuring out what makes you happy in life, and what you want or need to change in your relationship so that you can be happier.

If you want guidance and Energy Self-Defense tools to help you balance your own energy, we recommend that you read *"Energy Self-Defense for Women"* and *"Energy Self-Defense for Men"*. These two specific energy guides will teach you how to approach and affect both women's and men's energies in daily life.

When focusing on your relationship, there are some questions that you should ask both yourself and your spouse, to clarify what both of you want from your relationship, and how you and your partner can help contribute to making things work better.

Below are some questions that will hopefully make you think and make you more aware about where your personal boundaries are in your relationship, and what you should do about the whole situation if you are not happy.

There are no correct answers since we are all different. The right answers are those that you find yourself. At the end of this chapter you will find two mantras that will help you to better define your own energy, so that you can address your personal needs and hear your inner voice.

Questions:

- *Do you love and respect your partner deeply?*

- *Do you have enough freedom in your relationship?*

- *Are you taking care of too many things in the family and at home?*

- *Do you have to earn lots of money every month to pay the bills at home, and is this responsibility too big of a burden on your shoulders?*

- *Does your partner have a wandering eye, who can't resist handsome looking men/beautiful women without being turned on, and does this hurt you?*

- *Is your partner boring or egoistic and does he/she only show interest in their own things?*

- *Do you have money issues and are you or your partner more focused on spending money than earning money?*

- *Do you have problems with your children whether they are yours, mine or our children?*

- *Do you have ex-partners that cause trouble between you and your current partner?*

- *Is there room for emotions in your relationship and/or is your partner only focusing on having sex?*

- *Is there a good and balanced energy in your home and between you and your partner?*

- *Are you proud of your life, your partner, your children and yourself?*

Most problems in any relationship can be solved in an easy way when you send pure love energy to your spouse and your children, and to the whole family. It's amazing what love can do in a relationship and in a family. Most people calm down in a second and suddenly the children start to behave nicely and your partner wants to give you a loving kiss just because you are you. So, remember to send love to your loved ones every day. Then you will be happier and so will they. By using this mantra, you will send pure, radiating love energy:

"I now embrace myself in pink love energy to radiate love all around me."

or

"I now send pink love energy to 'X' to make him/her become more loving towards him/herself and towards me."

Also remember to dissolve all negative energy in your house whether it is between you as a couple or the whole family. You can do this by using the pink love energy and/or the white light/energy. By doing so the house will suddenly feel cleansed and it will be easier to breathe, even if there is still dust on the furniture. If you really want to raise the energy level in the house, place flowers in some of the rooms, and everybody will soon feel happier.

You can change the energy in your relationship and all around you in a positive way by using the following mantras:

"I now embrace myself
in a pure white light/energy
to dissolve all bad energies around me."

or

"I now send pure white light/energy to 'X'
to dissolve all bad energy around him/her."

By embracing yourself with white light/energy it cleanses out all negative energies in you. The white light/energy around you ensures that you won't be affected by any negative vibrations around you, and that all positive energy can easily get to you without problems.

By sending white light/energy to others, you dissolve all bad energies in and around them.

Go find your missing energy
(1 mantra)

If you are not happy, then go and find your missing energy which you can read about in this chapter.

When you lack a part of your personal energy, you will start behaving differently than before and become less successful. You might also find that you are not thinking as clearly as you used to, or your intuition has simply become weaker, etc.

To find your outstanding energy, you must:

1. First make a list of the things that you can no longer master in the same way as before. Have a look around you to see if your ex-partner, or some of the other people you know have suddenly become more successful in doing things that you have become less successful doing. Maybe it has been easy for you to earn money, and suddenly it's hard without any reason. The money issue should therefore be added to your list, and so on.

2. Now pull all your rightful energy back from the mentioned people and from your ex-partner. Draw your energy through a cleansing filter, so it's only your own energy that is returned to you and not some of the other energy that other people don't want to have anymore:

> *"I now pull all my rightful energy*
> *back to myself from 'X'*
> *– in a cleansed form –*
> *and I send all the rightful energy of 'X'*
> *out of my own energy field*
> *and return it to him/her."*

3. You will start to feel a change in you and in your behavior slowly over time, so don't despair; it may take some time to get your energy back, as it has to be pulled out of your ex-partner's or other people's energy systems, where it has existed for a long time as they thought it was their own energy.

It's very important that you reclaim your own rightful power and energy and get rid of other people's energy, which is why you should start to energetically clean up all your previous relationships by using the Energy Self-Defense tools described in this book.

Some people feed off of other people's energy while others are very giving. So be mindful of your missing energy and start searching for it in and around people who feed themselves through other people's energy and attention.

It's always a good idea to draw your energy back from everyone you know whether they are good or bad, because even if they don't actually have any of your energy, it doesn't hurt to play it safe and do the exercise anyways.

Balance in the relationship is a mutual project

Balance within any relationship is something that the couple must work on together since they know how they prefer things to be in their relationship.

If there is trouble in your relationship it's okay to ask others for help, but it usually doesn't change anything if only one person asks for help. Unlike many other types of relationships, a love relationship is a partnership with two equal "love investors", so if things aren't working between you, both of you should agree on how to recreate the balance between you and what to do next.

It's always good to talk to others and get advice, input and inspiration from the outside world on how to transform your relationship. To make things work in the long run, it's of even greater importance that you and your love partner are able to agree on the terms for how your relationship should be. Otherwise, there is no solid foundation to build a joint future on and it may all suddenly fall apart when you least expect it.

Using selected Energy Self-Defense tools can be of great help to sort things out in your relationship if you have certain issues that continue to come to the surface. By using the Energy Self-Defense tools to cleanse and balance the energy in your relationship, the underlying as well as the overall energy and the intention of each party will become crystal clear to both of you. It will then be possible for you and your love partner to both see and sense if there is a good and solid foundation to work on that can lead to something even better for you as a couple. It might also be crystal clear to you both if it's time to move on in different directions.

If you want to increase the likelihood that both you and your spouse positively want to stay in the relationship, then you should both follow the 5-Step Energy Self-Defense Plan for Love Couples later in this book to be sure there is a good foundation for you to continue being together as a love couple. It's a plan that can be used by all love couples if they have challenges in their relationship.

Please notice that if there is any kind of abuse and mental, emotional or physical violation in your relationship, it's a no-go for the relationship. Don't try to save such a relationship, because if you are the only one searching for help and advice from others, it will be very hard work for you, since you are probably the weakest or the abused one in the relationship.

People who ignore other people's needs rarely take their time to understand the dynamics in a relationship and would probably never read a book like this. So, with a partner who is selfish, you will be alone in the search to create balance in your relationship and you will constantly have an energy thief by your side who is searching for weak spots in your energy, so they can get energy from you without giving anything back.

Should you stay?
(6 mantras)

Infidelity can be perceived in many different ways.

Most people associate it with a physical action like kissing or having sex with someone other than their love partner, without having an agreement with their partner about it. Other people think it's the emotional intensity of the action that matters, so if there is love involved, it's considered infidelity.

To fantasize about or get turned on by another person than your love partner can also be perceived as infidelity and can be very hurtful to your love partner. So, it's not always the action itself that is the biggest problem. It's the hurtful feeling that your love partner is left with that will forever hurt them. You should therefore think long and hard before you jump into the "world of unfaithfulness", because it's a place where most people start to lie for the first time and always cover their tracks.

People addicted to drugs, alcohol, gambling, etc. usually have the same type of behavior and could also be perceived as being unfaithful to their partner. This type of individual is usually very focused on getting their next kick, fix or high outside of their love relationship, no matter how their partner feels about it. This is as hurtful to their love partner as if they were being intimate with another person. Typically, an addicted person normally cuts all ties and energies between themselves and their partner when they get the need to do certain things, without involving their love partner and without thinking about the consequences.

When the unfaithful person has got what he/she wants outside of the relationship, they usually come back home and want to reconnect with their love partner as if nothing has happened. Sometimes they even want to get more energy from their love partner, so they can get back on track, because they gave away their own energy and/or the mutual energy they had in them to another person or situation.

The energetic meaning of the term "infidelity" is when one person in a love relationship, without first consulting their love partner, starts acting like a single person and spends a large amount of their own and/or the couple's mutual energy to do something on their own, outside of the relationship, that will decrease the mutual energy in the relationship and will not benefit the couple.

Honesty, trust and freedom are very important ingredients in any love relationship, including "open relationships", where it's equally important that the couple agrees on the rules and how to behave.

Usually everything in and around the relationship is turned upside down if one person is being unfaithful to the other. Don't expect things to settle and balance right away. It can take a **very** long time to balance the energy in the relationship after this trust has been broken, even if both parties want to continue being together.

If your partner is being unfaithful to you, you have to decide whether you should stay or leave, which can be a very tough decision especially if you are very angry at him/her right now.

No matter what you decide to do, we recommend that you follow the 5-Step Energy Self-Defense Plan for Love Couples mentioned later in this book. If you decide to leave your partner, **do not** go through step 5, where you share your love with each other.

If you want to keep your partner's energies away from you, you can use this powerful mantra that will make it clear to everybody around you what you think of him/her:

"I now place a thick wall
of blue boundary-setting energy
between me and 'X'
to separate our energies
and to keep 'X' away from me."

However, there will be a much better flow in everything you do if you go through step 1, 2, 3 and 4, in the right order, in the 5-Step Energy Self-Defense Plan for Love Couples to make sure your energies are separated more profoundly from each other.

When you cleanse the energies in your relationship, you don't have to cleanse your partner's energy, unless you hope it will lead to something good. It should be your partner's own responsibility to do that. Say the following mantras, because it's important that you focus on you and not on your relationship, to be happy again.

Step 1: Sort your energies

"I now pull all my rightful energy
back to myself from 'X'
– in a cleansed form –
and I send all the rightful energy of 'X'
out of my own energy field
and return it to him/her."

Step 2: Let go of the past

*"I now bless all people, places
and experiences from my past and/or present
and neutralize the energies between us
with Divine and positive energy."*

Step 3: Dissolve all bad energies in and around you

*"I now embrace myself
in a pure white light/energy
to dissolve all bad energies around me
and my relationship."*

Step 4: Find your own truth

*"I now forgive myself and 'X'
for what happened.
I now let go of all that happened
and create space for new positive
experiences in my life."*

and

*"I now place a thick wall
of blue boundary-setting energy
between me and 'X'
to separate our energies
and to keep 'X' away from me."*

If you decide to stay in your relationship, then you can continue the cleansing process by focusing on cleansing and balancing the energy in your relationship – hopefully together with your love partner – but not until **after** you have focused on cleansing and balancing your own energy. In that case you should follow the 5-Step Energy Self-Defense Plan for Love Couples mentioned later in the book.

The same goes for you, if you are the unfaithful one in the relationship, but before doing that, we recommend that you read *"Energy Self-Defense for Women"* or *"Energy Self-Defense for Men"* as you apparently need to find yourself, before you focus on saving your relationship. Who knows, maybe your existing relationship is not right for you, since you have a continuous need to cross the invisible boundaries of your relationship searching for someone or something else – or for yourself.

Start searching for yourself and find out how to meet your own needs, because then you can hopefully attract a partner that fulfils your needs and vice versa. Being conscious and honest about who you are and what you want in life makes it much easier for you to attract those things and conditions.

Do you stay because of the children?

(2 mantras)

Even in modern times where most people have learned how to express themselves and be honest with their loved ones, there are still many couples who don't love each other anymore and choose to stay together (but **not** as love couples), just because of their children.

If this also applies to you, we warmly recommend that you take the time to think things through. Ask yourself if this was what you would want your own parents to have done when you were a child, if you knew that they no longer loved each other, and that they might be suffering and not truly happy just because they wanted to protect you, their loving child, from the facts of life.

Even though most children want their parents to stay together forever, because parents represent two different sides of the children, then also ask yourself if this is what your children would want for you, if they knew how you felt. Also think of how much power you give to your children even if they have never asked for it and may not even know how bad things are in your relationship, simply because you fake every day by pretending that everything is okay, even if it's not.

Staying together as a couple without loving each other, because of the children, can be a very high price to pay for all involved parties, because the children are often playing a more powerful role in their parents' life, where the parents focus on exchanging energies with them instead of with their spouse, because the children are now their closest and most dear ones. This scenario is not healthy for any child because of the big responsibility for making their parents feel happy that is suddenly placed on the children's shoulders.

And what about love? Is this the kind of love between adults that you want to show to your children, where they learn on an unconsciously level to accept that things don't have to be optimal in their future love relationship. Always remember that you are the most important and influential role models for your children.

If you cannot afford to leave your partner, or there are other reasons why you cannot separate, then try and make an arrangement where you involve your children in the separation process. Your children will usually come up with good solutions on how to balance things in daily life, because they know both of you very well and love you both. Therefore, they will try to make things as fair as possible for everyone.

If you decide to split up eventually, then better to do it sooner than later, because it's much easier to split up your energies and go in different directions if you are still on friendly terms.

In case you decide to stay together for certain reasons, you are recommended to sort and balance your energies in your "relationship" daily by using the following mantras.

Step 1: Sort your energies

"I now pull all my rightful energy
back to myself from 'X'
– in a cleansed form –
and I send all the rightful energy of 'X'
out of my own energy field
and return it to him/her."

Step 2: Dissolve all bad energies in and around you and your children's other parent

"I now embrace myself
in a pure white light/energy
to dissolve all bad energies around me
and between me and 'X'."

The Energy Self-Defense Protection Tools

(1 mantra)

Now that you have a good idea of what you want in your relationship, this section will give you the practical steps to protect and balance your energy when you are with your love partner and want to defend yourself.

If you feel that your relationship is a fight in itself and that you have no support from your partner who is manipulating, being disrespectful or not being kind to you, you should protect your energy in the most effective way possible by using the following Energy Self-Defense Protection Tools again and again.

You can also use the Energy Self-Defense Protection Tools to protect your relationship against bad energy coming from others, who want to separate you from each other. For example, a jealous ex-partner, or other people who don't support your mutual love:

1. First, you have to be energetically persistent and you should not start using the Energy Self-Defense Protection Tools until your opponent, who might be your partner, thinks that you have given up and are at your weakest. The less attention and energy you give them, the more of their own energy they have to use in their fight against you.

2. If your partner or other people cross your boundaries in one way or another, you can see for yourself that the boundary-crossing person is burned with a pure flame

of fire, as if they had been burned to ashes. There must not be a single part of the person's energy that escapes the flames of truth.

3. You can also see for yourself that all the resistance that other people send or have sent in your direction changes character from being negative and dark to being a positive, bright and joyous energy which benefits you.

   If the resistance comes from your partner, the energy that is converted into positive energy should **only** benefit you.

   If the resistance comes from other people who don't support your relationship, then the energy that is converted into positive energy should benefit your relationship.

4. If you don't want to convert negative energy into positive energy for the benefit of you and/or your relationship, you can use your thought power to send the resistance back to the sender, so that they have to deal with the negative energy themselves.

5. The final and most effective Energy Self-Defense Protection Tool is to embrace your opponent with a blue boundary-setting bubble that will lock them inside the bubble with their own boundary-crossing energy, so they can get a strong taste of their own unpleasant behavior. If it doesn't make them respect your personal boundaries, then place a tight ring of violet transforming energy around the blue bubble, which will automatically transform the person in a positive direction, possibly through less pleasant experiences, if he/she manages to get out of the blue boundary-setting energy bubble.

   If and when, the person gets out of the blue boundary-setting energy bubble and enters the violet energy ring, you cannot be sure what will happen and in which way. All you know is that your opponent has now reached the transforming violet energy of their own free will by crossing your personal boundaries and the color blue that you placed around the person to protect yourself.

With this approach, the violet transforming energy has not been sent directly on the person, because you are **not** allowed to send transforming violet energy directly on other people and animals, because it can cause a very fast, powerful and intense transformation that is totally out of control. However, if you want a fast and powerful transformation in certain areas of your life that cause you trouble, you can send violet transforming energy on the situation, place or relationship. Just not on other people and animals:

"I now embrace 'X'
with a blue boundary-setting bubble
and a tight ring of violet transforming energy
around the blue bubble
to make 'X' respect
my personal boundaries."

The 5-Step Energy Self-Defense Plan for Love Couples
(6 mantras)

The purpose of this 5-Step plan is to give you some concrete advice and guidance on what to do and how to do it, as well as what to expect in your relationship as you begin manifesting energy in the right way. It is recommended that both you and your partner go through this 5-Step plan, but you should each do so individually.

Here is an overview of the 5-Step Energy Self-Defense Plan for Love Couples:

Step 1: Sort your energies
Step 2: Let go of the past
Step 3: Dissolve all bad energies between you and your love partner
Step 4: Find your own truth in your relationship
Step 5: Share your love with each other

Now let's go through each step in details.

Step 1: Sort your energies

First you should sort your energies so that both of you get the opportunity to stay strong in your respective energies. Repeat the energy sorting mantra below in your mind or say it out loud as many times a day as possible. It cannot be repeated too much.

By using this mantra and separating your personal energies day and night, you will soon feel whether you miss each other deeply and want to be together or not. You will get a very strong feeling in your body, mind, spirit and emotions that indicates whether you should stay together or not. It will also be visible to both of you if you are still attracted to each other, almost as if you have been away from each other for a long time and can't wait to come home and be together again:

> *"I now pull all my rightful energy back to myself*
> *from my love partner*
> *– in a cleansed form –*
> *and I send all the rightful energy*
> *of my love partner*
> *out of my own energy field*
> *and return it to him/her."*

Even if you get a very good result within a few days by just doing this, you should **not** stop here. Continue the entire plan by following the other four steps and exercises in the 5-Step Energy Self-Defense Plan to ensure long-lasting results in your relationship.

Step 2: Let go of the past

Many people have a hard time letting go of their past, and it's therefore extremely important to clean all energies that are related to the past in both of you, as well as in your current and previous relationship(s).

It could be bad experiences that you have had in your relationship(s). It could also be death, or trouble in the family and other personal challenges, etc., that are still haunting you. Many different types of experiences can have a very negative impact on your personality and relationship today that will impact your balance in daily life without you noticing it, simply because you have become so used to problems in your life.

You should therefore focus on letting go of the past by using this divine Energy Self-Defense mantra:

> *"I now bless all people, places*
> *and experiences from my past and/or present*
> *and neutralize the energies between us*
> *with Divine and positive energy."*

Step 3: Dissolve all bad energies between you and your love partner

There is a reason you are going through these steps so remember to be patient and follow through on all of the steps in this plan.

Just imagine how you would feel if you stopped following the 5-Step Energy Self-Defense Plan after step 1 because you think that all of the problems are solved, and then they suddenly come back with full power on day 4, simply because you hoped for a very quick and positive response to this energy sorting exercise?

Your relationship problems did not happen overnight, so be patient as these exercises take time.

You should not give up before you've started, but you should also not think that you nailed it just because you had one good result. So don't be naive. The good result is just an indicator that tells you that you are on the right path and should continue to cleanse and balance your energies.

The importance of dissolving all bad energies that have ever found their way into your relationship should not be underestimated. To create a new and positive foundation in your relationship demands a thorough cleansing from both you and your partner's side – almost like having a full house makeover where all the doors and window panels are removed and replaced with new ones.

If your partner doesn't want to participate in the cleansing process, it will of course take a much longer time for you to clean the whole "house" alone, and you will never be able to dissolve, clean and balance all of your partner's personal stuff from the past. Since it's personal stuff, it has to be treated like that, so you cannot walk the path for your spouse and create inner balance for him/her.

You can be there for your spouse and you can support and listen to him/her, but you might run the risk of being very disappointed during the process, if your partner doesn't show any interest in digging deep into personal issues of the past that you can't do anything about. In that case you can still decide to go through the whole 5-Step Energy Self-Defense Plan for Love Couples yourself without your partner assisting you, since it's usually better to do something to change the situation than to do nothing at all.

Perhaps you going through the 5-Step Energy Self-Defense Plan alone will motivate your partner afterwards to do the same, if your partner notices a positive change around you and your energy. Who knows?

Repeat the following mantra as often as you can to dissolve all bad energies in your relationship:

*"I now embrace myself,
my love partner and our relationship
in a pure white light/energy
to dissolve all bad energies around me,
my love partner and our relationship."*

By embracing yourself, your love partner and your relationship with white light/energy you cleanse out all negative energies in and around you both and in your relationship. The white light/energy will act as a layer of divine protection around you and will make sure there is no room for dishonesty and negative vibrations and energies around you, so you can get in contact with your inner truth as well as your mutual truth in the relationship.

If you and your love partner have supported each other and cooperated during the whole cleansing and dissolving process, it's now time to reconnect and embrace each other with love. Therefore, skip step 4 and instead go directly to step 5. If not, then continue with step 4.

Step 4: Find your own truth in your relationship

If **you** have done all the energy sorting and balancing yourself with no or little support from your partner, there is still some work to do for you to make sure that you are both happy with the new energetic foundation that **you** have created in your relationship.

In this phase, it is very important to be sure that how things are in your relationship today is also how you want them to be in the future. If you allow your love partner to get full access to your personal energy now without him/her showing any further engagement in the overall cleansing and balancing project, there is not much hope for your relationship. Unfortunately, this is how things are because of your partner's lack of involvement.

It's therefore important that you take your time to forgive yourself and your partner both for what happened in the past and for his/her lack of involvement in the development of your relationship, and let go of the past and the present, and all of the unsatisfactory conditions in your relationship, which can be done by saying the following mantra:

> *"I now forgive myself and my love partner*
> *for what happened.*
> *I now let go of all that happened*
> *and create space for new positive experiences*
> *in my life, in my partner's life*
> *and in our relationship."*

If your love partner has **not** supported you in the cleansing process at all and doesn't show you the respect that you deserve, and if he/she doesn't allow you to stay in your own space where you are in full contact with your own source, you should separate your energies for a couple of days or more where you and your partner will have some time to decide whether you want to stay in the relationship or not.

It's very important that you allow yourself and your partner to take the time to find your own truth in the relationship, without risking falling into your old behavior patterns.

Usually, this is the toughest part of the 5-Step Energy Self-Defense Plan for Love Couples, because you will have to split up your energies by placing a thick and boundary-setting energy between you, so you cannot get access to each other's energies while you take your time to think through what you want your relationship to be like in the future.

You can separate your energies by using this mantra:

> *"I now place a thick wall*
> *of blue boundary-setting energy*
> *between me and my love partner to make sure*
> *that both of us get our own space*
> *to think things through."*

If both of you feel bad during this process because you miss the close contact between you, then there is nothing to be scared of. Then you know that everything will be fine and that you will both do your best to make things work in your relationship. It can actually be healthy for both of you to miss each other once in a while to be better able to respect and worship your relationship.

If one of you likes the sudden "freedom" from your love partner a lot, there is for sure something for this person to think about – and maybe there is something that needs to be changed in your relationship. So, if you decide to stay together after the separating process, you should take the time to talk things through to find a new and better balance in your relationship that leaves room for personal space, freedom, balance, joy and happiness for each of you.

Step 5: Share your love with each other

When you know for sure that all you want is to continue your relationship, there is only one thing to do, if your love partner feels the same. You should of course share all your love with each other and feel the love go deep into your bones.

When sharing your love with each other, you should be as one rather than two separate energies. You should focus on the mutual energy in your relationship, so you will both benefit from the love energy as individuals and as a love couple.

Say the following mantra or see in your mind's eye that it happens:

*"I now embrace myself, my love partner
and our relationship in pink love energy
to activate and radiate love in our relationship
and between us,
so we can become more loving and respectful
towards each other."*

If both you and your love partner say the mantra, you will both help to improve love, honesty and respectfulness in your relationship. There is no difference in the energy and you will get the same effect whether it's just one of you or both of you who embrace your relationship in love energy. However, the feeling of love between you will grow much stronger when both of you focus on sending love to each other.

Thank you for reading

If you want to know more about how to protect and defend your personal energy in your life, please visit our website:

www.energyselfdefense.com

Here you will find information about our collection of helpful energy guides in our Energy Self-Defense series. We suggest that you begin with *"Energy Self-Defense for Women"* and *"Energy Self-Defense for Men"* where you will benefit from advice on how to achieve a more balanced life on a personal level. You can also participate in our online courses.

To learn more about the authors, please feel free to visit our other websites:

www.sennovpartners.com

www.annisennov.com

www.carstensennov.com

We hope that you are happy with what you learned from reading this Energy Self-Defense guide, and remember to go back to the Mantras often and integrate them into your daily habits.

Please tell your family, friends, colleagues and neighbors about our Energy Self-Defense series, so that we can hopefully work collectively to make this a better world to live in for all living beings.

A good way to spread the word about how to take care of your own energy is by giving *"The Little Energy Guide 1"*, which is a pocket size energy guide, to those you love and care about.

Finally, you can spread good energy by rating and commenting on this book at the site where you bought it, as well as on Anni Sennov's author page at **Goodreads.com**.

If you want inspiration on creating more freedom and personal space in your relationship, what you can do to feel more inspired to do something extra for your love partner, and making your relationship more interesting and alive, we kindly recommend for you to read Anni's book *"Love, Sex and Attraction – A Short Guide to a Successful Relationship"*. Here you will get lots of tips on how to be more realistic and optimistic as well as how to improve the energy and the attraction in your relationship.

As previously mentioned in this book, you are also recommended to read *"Spirit Mates – The New Time Relationship"*, if you want to know how easy things can be in a love relationship when you are together with your one and only love partner.

Finally, we recommend that you read our book *"SPIRIT MATES – How to Find Your Soul Mate Version 2.0 – Your Ultimate Love Partner"*, that our readers have been asking for for a long time, and which includes 10 real-life spirit mates love stories. This book explains how remarkable life can be when you are with your one and only spirit mate and various ways you can meet each other, etc.

Loving regards,

Anni & Carsten Sennov